WHY DOES IT HAPPEN?: PLANETS, OUTER SPACE AND THE ATMOSPHERE

SPEEDY
PUBLISHING

Speedy Publishing LLC
40 E. Main St. #1156
Newark, DE 19711
www.speedypublishing.com

A planet is an astronomical object that orbits the sun, has sufficient mass to be round, or nearly round and is not a satellite of another object.

PLANETS

Our solar system consists of the sun, eight planets, moons, many dwarf planets, an asteroid belt, comets, meteors, and others. The eight planets that orbit the sun are: Mercury, Venus, Earth, Mars, Jupiter, Saturn, Uranus, Neptune.

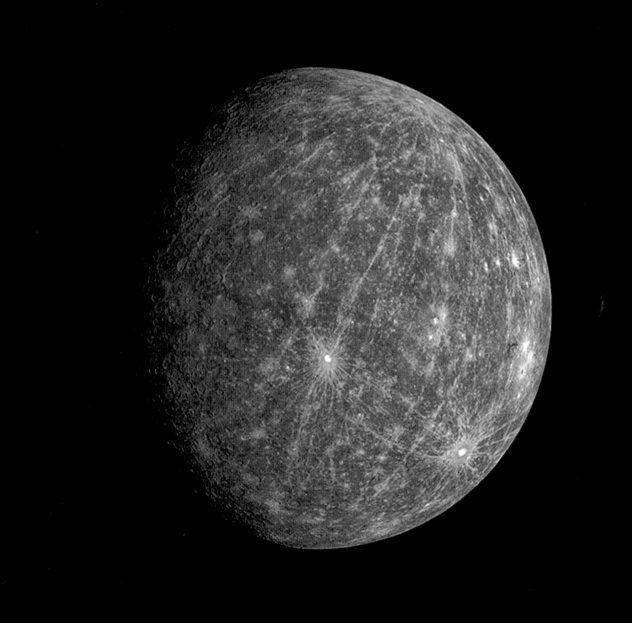

Mercury is the smallest and closest planet to the Sun. Mercury zips around the sun faster than any other planet. Mercury has the thinnest atmosphere of any planet in the solar system.

Venus is the second planet from the Sun. Venus is a terrestrial planet and is sometimes called Earth's "sister planet" because of their similar size, mass, proximity to the Sun and bulk composition.

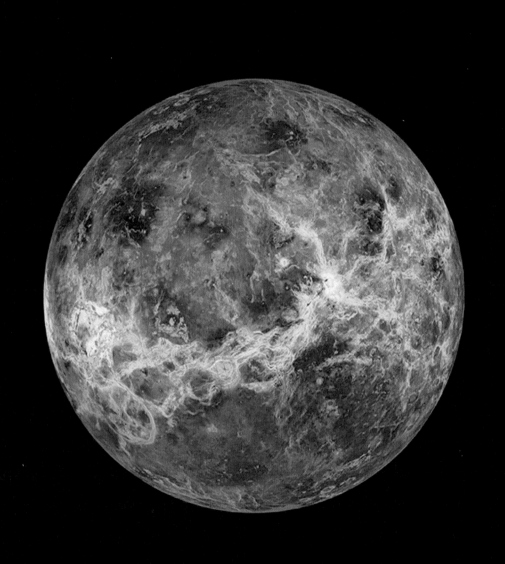

Earth is the third planet from the Sun and the densest planet in the Solar System. The earliest life on Earth arose at least 3.5 billion years ago.

Mars is the fourth planet from the Sun and the second smallest planet in the Solar System. Mars has many massive volcanoes and is home to Olympus Mons, the largest volcano in our solar system.

Jupiter is the fifth planet from the Sun and the largest planet in the Solar System. Jupiter has at least 67 moons. This includes the four large moons called the Galilean moons that were first discovered by Galileo Galilei in 1610.

Saturn is the sixth planet from the Sun and the second largest in the Solar System. Saturn is a gas giant made up mostly of hydrogen and helium.

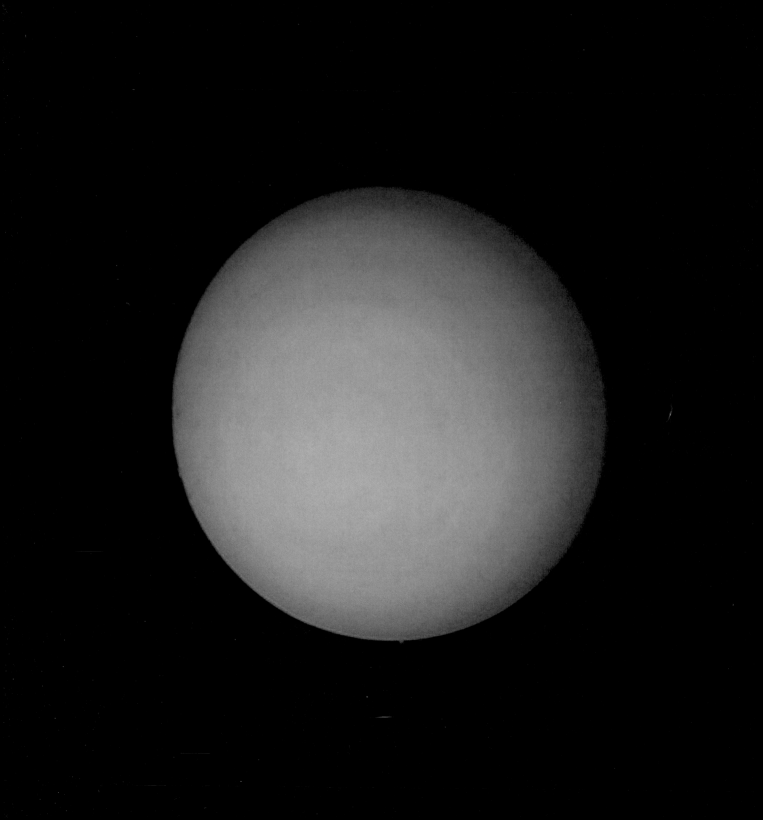

Uranus is the seventh planet from the Sun. Uranus is the coldest planetary atmosphere in the Solar System.

Neptune is the eighth and farthest planet from the Sun in the Solar System. Neptune is a large, water planet with a blue hydrogen-methane atmosphere and faint rings.

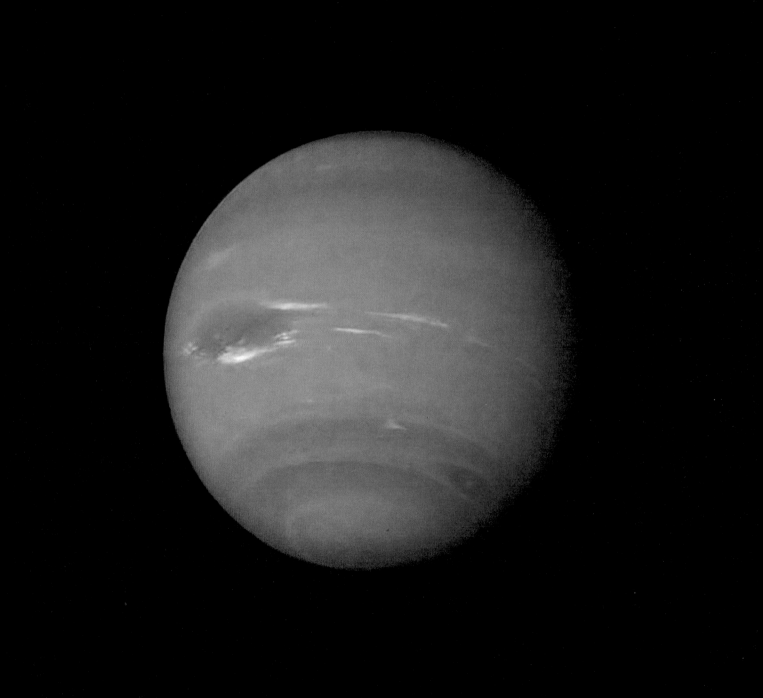

OUTER SPACE

Outer space is the void that exists between celestial bodies, including the Earth. Outer space is a vacuum with no breathable air or pressure.

ATMOSPHERE

The atmosphere is a thin layer of gases that surrounds the Earth. The atmosphere is a mixture of nitrogen, oxygen and other gases that surrounds Earth. It seals the planet and protects us from the vacuum of space.

Made in the USA
Monee, IL
27 July 2021